THEN AND THERE SERIES
CREATED BY MARJORIE REEVES
GENERAL EDITOR: JOHN FINES

Mary Queen of Scots

Second Edition

W. K. RITCHIE

Illustrated from contemporary sources

Longman

LONGMAN GROUP UK LIMITED,
*Longman House, Burnt Mill, Harlow,
Essex CM20 2JE, England
and Associated Companies throughout the world.*

*Published in the United States of America by
Longman Inc., New York.*

First published 1979
Second Edition 1990

*Set in 11/13 point Rockwell Light (Linotron)
Produced by Longman Group (F.E.). Limited
Printed in Hong Kong*

ISBN 0 582 03404 3

Acknowledgements

We are grateful to the following for permission to reproduce photographs:
Bibliotheque Nationale, pages 18, 34; Bodleian Library, page 11; British
Library, pages 5, 9, 29, 58; Camera Press, page 16 (photo: Pierre
Berger); from: Frere-Cook: *The Decorative Arts of the Mariner*, Cassell,
1966, page 14; Crown Copyright photograph: Public Record Office, Lon-
don, pages 44, 47; Lord Egremont, page 27; National Galleries of Scot-
land, pages 23, 36, 42; National Portrait Gallery, pages 7, 54; by Courtesy
of the Board of Trustees, Victoria & Albert Museum, pages 52, 56.
Cover. Miniature of Mary, Queen of Scots by Clouet. Reproduced by
Gracious Permission of Her Majesty the Queen.

Contents

To the reader

This book is about one of the most famous women who ever lived. Books, plays, films, an opera and a ballet have all been written about her. Ask almost any group of people and you will be sure that one of them has heard of Mary Queen of Scots. This book may help you to understand why.

But this book is not just about a famous queen. It tells you also about the time in which she lived, especially about the great changes in religion that were taking place which still affect the lives of people today.

Words printed in **thick black** are explained in the Glossary which begins on page 61.

1 A child queen

Royal birth

Below is an engraving of Linlithgow Palace in West Lothian in Scotland. It is only a ruin today, but hundreds of years ago kings and queens lived here. On the 8th of December 1542 there was great excitement in the palace with the news that the Queen had just had a baby. Many were sorry, however, that the baby was not a boy. At this time people did not like the idea of being ruled by a woman, and as the King and Queen had no other children, it was likely that this little girl would be the next ruler of Scotland.

The baby's father, King James V, was many miles away at Falkland Palace in Fife, lying very ill. In fact, he was dying. Recently he had quarrelled with King Henry VIII of England and his army had been beaten in battle at Solway Moss, near Carlisle. Some of his best soldiers had

An engraving of Linlithgow Palace. Can you see why kings and queens might feel safe living here?

been killed and many of his nobles taken prisoner. So, when news came that he had a daughter and not a son to succeed him, James was so disappointed, it is said, that he cried, 'Alas! It came with a lass and it will pass with a lass.' He was thinking of how his family, the Stewarts, had come to rule Scotland through a 'lass', Marjorie, daughter of King Robert the Bruce, and was afraid that they would now stop ruling Scotland with a 'lass', his little daughter, Mary. On the 14th of December 1542 James V died, leaving Mary to become Queen of Scots when she was less than a week old.

Henry VIII steps in

Since Mary was only a baby, a **regent** would have to rule the country. Two men said they should be chosen: **Cardinal** David Beaton, who was James V's chief adviser, and the Earl of Arran, who was a distant relative. Neither would give way.

Rulers in other countries were very interested in who should become Regent of Scotland. European rulers supported one or other of the two most powerful rulers of the time: the King of France, or the Emperor (Charles V), who ruled not only the Empire in Germany and Italy, but also Spain and the Low Countries. As an old enemy of France, the English King sided with the Emperor, and since England was the 'Auld Enemy' of Scotland, the Scots kept up their 'Auld **Alliance**' with France. Each side was always afraid of the other becoming more powerful. Since Scotland was now without a strong ruler, England and the Emperor were much stronger than France alone. So the French wanted to keep Scotland as a useful **ally** and the English wanted to take Scotland away.

The little Queen's mother, Mary of Guise, was French so she naturally wanted to keep up the Auld Alliance. And so did Cardinal Beaton. Henry VIII of England therefore was determined to stop Beaton from being made Regent and to get the Earl of Arran appointed instead. Arran was

Henry VIII of England, c. 1542. What is it about his appearance that tells you he was used to getting his own way?

also in favour of Henry's plan for a marriage of the little Queen of Scots to the King's young son, Edward, who would one day succeed him as King of England. In this way the two countries would be united, with Scotland under English control.

Another problem in all this complicated pattern was to do with religion. Henry VIII had made himself head of the

7

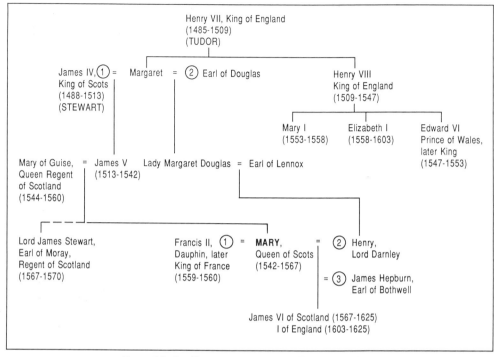

Henry VII, King of England
(1485-1509)
(TUDOR)

James IV, (1) = Margaret = (2) Earl of Douglas
King of Scots
(1488-1513)
(STEWART)

Henry VIII
King of England
(1509-1547)

Mary I
(1553-1558)

Elizabeth I
(1558-1603)

Edward VI
Prince of Wales,
later King
(1547-1553)

Mary of Guise, = James V
Queen Regent   (1513-1542)
of Scotland
(1544-1560)

Lady Margaret Douglas = Earl of Lennox

Lord James Stewart,
Earl of Moray,
Regent of Scotland
(1567-1570)

Francis II, (1) = MARY, = (2) Henry,
Dauphin, later   Queen of Scots   Lord Darnley
King of France   (1542-1567)
(1559-1560)

= (3) James Hepburn,
Earl of Bothwell

James VI of Scotland (1567-1625)
I of England (1603-1625)

From this family tree, can you see that Mary's father, James V, was a
nephew of Henry VIII? This made Henry VIII Mary's great-uncle. Use
this family tree to see how other people mentioned in this book are
related to each other. The dates show when the Kings and Queens
reigned.

Church in England instead of the Pope, and many people
in England favoured the Protestant ideas of Martin Luther
and even Ulrich Zwingli. There were Protestants in Scotland, too, as we shall see, but most of the powerful people
wanted to stay with the old Roman Catholic religion, as did
France and the Empire.

To carry out his scheme, Henry sent back those Scottish
nobles captured at Solway Moss who promised to help him
take over Scotland. Henry's plan worked. The Earl of
Arran was made Regent and talks started for the marriage
of Mary to Edward.

Then things began to go wrong for Henry. With help
from France, Beaton and Mary of Guise managed to bribe

the Earl of Arran to side with them. Some of Henry's Scottish nobles were locked up and the baby Queen was sent to Stirling Castle in case Henry tried to kidnap her.

'The rough wooing'

Henry VIII was not used to his plans being upset. On the 10th of April 1544 he ordered the Earl of Hertford to invade Scotland with an army of 10,000 men. These were Hertford's orders:

> 'Put all to fire and sword, burn down Edinburgh town, beat down the castle, **sack** Holyrood house and as many towns and villages about Edinburgh as you can; sack Leith, . . . putting man, woman and child to fire and sword without exception where any resist you.'

Part of a drawing of Edinburgh done in 1544. Though many of the roofs are damaged, notice that the walls of the houses are still standing.

This was how Henry VIII tried to persuade the Scots to let his son marry their Queen. An old-fashioned word for a man trying to persuade a woman to marry him is 'wooing'. So the Scots spoke about Henry's clumsy methods as 'the rough wooing'.

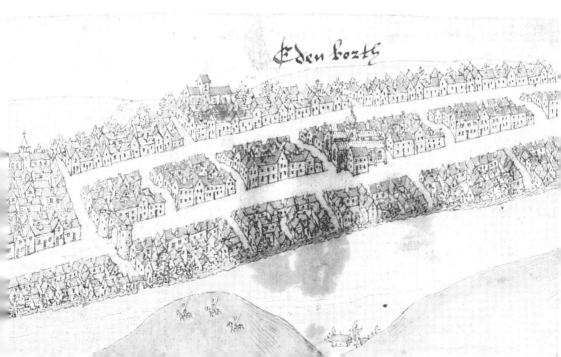

Murder at St Andrews

Henry VIII now tried to conquer Scotland another way, by murder. His chief enemy, Cardinal Beaton, had many enemies in Scotland, some of whom hated him for his bad behaviour as leader of the Church there. In 1546 Henry secretly paid them to go ahead with their plan to kill him. Their leader was Norman Leslie, a Fife landowner, whom Beaton had cheated out of some land.

In May 1546 the Cardinal was living in his castle at St Andrews, protected by its stout walls and the sea on three sides. Early one morning Leslie and his friends entered the castle disguised as workmen. Before the guards could raise the alarm they had quickly taken control of the place. They found Beaton in his bedroom with the door blocked up with furniture. When Leslie ordered his men to burn down the door Beaton unlocked it. Inside they found the Cardinal, cowering in a chair. 'I am a priest!' he cried. 'Ye will not slay me!' But they did, then hung his body upside down from the castle walls.

The siege of St Andrew's Castle

The murder of Cardinal Beaton did Henry VIII no good, however. It only made Mary of Guise all the more determined to keep up the French alliance and prevent her daughter's marriage to Henry's son. But when the Regent Arran ordered the arrest of Beaton's murderers, they locked themselves in St Andrew's Castle, knowing the Cardinal had left plenty of stores and ammunition.

The siege of St Andrew's Castle lasted over a year and only ended when, in July 1547, a French army landed with cannon and after six hours shot away one of the castle towers and battered down the south wall. Many of the castle's defenders were then taken away to serve as galley slaves in the French ships. So Cardinal Beaton's death had been avenged and once more English plans to conquer Scotland had been foiled.

The Battle of Pinkie – 10th September 1547

By this time, however, Henry VIII was dead and the nine-year-old Edward VI had become King in January 1547 with his uncle, the Earl of Hertford – or the Duke of Somerset as he had become – ruling England on his behalf. At the end of August 1547 Somerset began 'the rough wooing' yet again, with a fleet of ships sailing up the Scottish coast to supply his army of 16,000 men on its march to Edinburgh.

This time the Scottish leaders were determined to halt the invaders with a well-equipped army of 20,000 men and plenty of cannon. About six miles east of Edinburgh they took up positions on the left bank of the River Esk near Musselburgh. From their camp on the other side of the river at Prestonpans, Somerset spread out his men as far as Falside Hill to the south-west. You can see the positions of the two armies on the map below.

In this sketch of the Battle of Pinkie you are looking southwards from the Firth of Forth. Notice the two armies drawn up in their battle formations with flags flying and heavy cannon. The English are on the left and top left, the Scots, bottom right. Look for the English ships off shore. What made the Scots an easy target for the English gunners on land and sea?

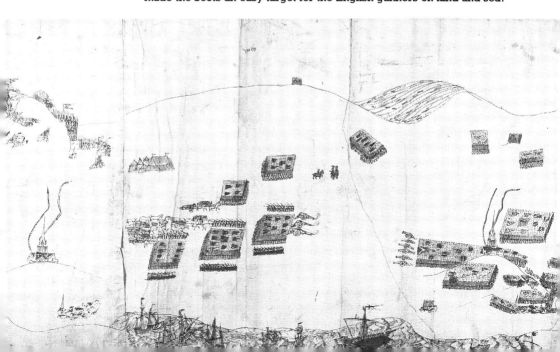

The English made up for their smaller numbers with better discipline and greater experience. The foot soldiers, armed with **pikes**, were supported by archers and about 4,000 heavy **cavalry**, some of whom were trained to shoot a kind of gun known as an arquebus as they rode.

The Earl of Arran was a most uninspiring general and many of the other Scottish nobles were unreliable too, having already fought for the English. Most of the men had never fought together before, and the cavalry were so badly disciplined that some broke ranks before the fighting even started.

The Battle of Pinkie, as it was called, began early on the 10th of September 1547 and lasted all morning. As a result of a misunderstanding, two wings of the Scottish army marched into each other, and in the confusion were easily mown down by the heavy English cavalry, supported by cannon-fire both on land and from the ships off shore.

The slaughter was terrible. The Earl of Arran fled and the Scottish army simply collapsed. By one o'clock the battle was all over with the Scots scattered in every direction. The whole area was strewn with corpses, 'as cattle in a well stocked pasture field', wrote an English observer. It was almost as terrible a defeat for the Scots as the Battle of Flodden in 1513.

Royal refugee

All the time, however, little Queen Mary was safe, first in Stirling Castle, and then at Inchmahome **Priory** on an island in the Lake of Menteith. But her mother thought that nowhere in Scotland would she be safe from the English. So she asked the French King to send more troops to Scotland and to arrange for Mary to be sent to France. In June 1548, while their men besieged the English based at Haddington, Scottish and French leaders nearby agreed that Mary should be sent to France and later marry the **Dauphin**, the French King's son.

The ships which had brought the French troops now

sailed round Scotland to Dumbarton Castle on the River Clyde, where Mary was taken safely on board. In this power game between France and England while Mary was a child queen of five-years-old, France had won the first round.

Things to do

1. Why do you think people were worried about having a ruler who was female? Why was it bad in their eyes to have a sovereign who was a child? We might think very differently about this in our day, but make a list of how they might have argued in the sixteenth century.

2. Why did Henry VIII behave the way he did towards Scotland? Do you think he felt he was doing the right thing when he invaded? Try to get some more information about what happened between England and Scotland after this time. What do people feel about this today?

3. Why did Scotland get involved with France rather than with England? Look at a map and see whether you can see what were the advantages and the disadvantages of the Auld Alliance.

4. Do you think these early experiences would have an effect on Mary, all this happening before she was six? How do you think it might have influenced her as she began to grow up?

2 A French upbringing

At the French court

In this French galley note the sails (not in use) and the oars, rowed usually by galley slaves. Why was a ship like this not suitable for sailing in stormy northern seas?

Mary's ships took her to France round the west of Ireland to avoid English pirates. Keeping her company were four young friends about her own age: Mary Beaton, Mary Seton, Mary Fleming and Mary Livingston, her 'Four Maries'. The crossing was very stormy, but after eighteen days at sea, Mary landed at Roscoff, safe and sound.

Mary spent the next thirteen years in France. Every-

Pick out places mentioned in the text.

where she was treated with great respect and friendliness. Her French grandmother, Duchess Antoinette of Guise, introduced her to the French King, Henry II, who liked her straightaway. The King had three children of his own, Francis the Dauphin, aged five, and two little girls, Elisabeth and Claude. The Queen of France, Catherine de Medici, was also pleased with Mary and said, 'Our little Scottish queen has but to smile to turn all French heads.'

Mary was brought up with the royal children. Kings at this time travelled about their country to see that it was properly governed and to live off the rent paid by their tenants. The royal castles where Mary lived were truly splendid. Though protected by turrets and high walls, their large windows showed that they were built not only for defence. The interiors were magnificent, with floors of

15

Fountainebleau, one of the many beautiful castles where Mary lived with members of the French royal family. From its many large windows what do you think it was like inside?

polished wood or marble, walls covered with bright **tapestries**, and ceilings decorated with gaily painted panels or elaborate plasterwork.

Everything at the French court was for show, especially the clothes. As a queen Mary had to look her best. In 1551 she had sixteen dresses made, all of velvet with silk or satin linings, and with more than ten pairs of shoes to match.

Much time at court was spent in entertainment. Mary enjoyed riding, hunting, archery, and a new sport, called tennis. She loved to watch with other ladies while gentlemen dressed up in armour and fought mock battles, known as tournaments. Indoor pastimes included cards, chess and **backgammon**. Mary also learned to sew and enjoyed doing embroidery for the rest of her days. Everyone at court was expected to compose songs and poems, and so Mary wrote verses with the help of a famous court poet, Pierre Ronsard. She was taught to play the **lute** and other musical instruments. Since there was always dancing at the French court, a dancing master showed her the steps of the slow and stately pavane and of the livelier jig and galliard.

Mary spent a lot of time in the school-room too. Apart from French, which she spoke nearly all the time, she learned English, Spanish and Italian. Like other educated people at this time she had also to know ancient Greek and enough Latin to be able to speak it. When she was thirteen, she gave a Latin speech at the court, and her uncle wrote to her mother:

> 'Your daughter is improving, and increasing day by day in stature, goodness, beauty, wisdom and worth. She is so perfect in all things . . . that the like of her is not to be seen in this realm . . . the King has taken so great a liking to her that he spends much of his time chatting with her, . . . and she knows well how to entertain him, with pleasant and sensible subjects of conversation as if she were a woman of five and twenty.'

Royal wedding

Meanwhile, things were happening outside France that were to change Mary's life. In England Edward VI died in 1553 and his Roman Catholic half-sister, Mary Tudor, became Queen. Her marriage to the King of Spain now made them firm allies in a war against France. To bring Scotland even more under French control, Mary of Guise replaced the Earl of Arran as Regent herself and arranged for Mary to marry the Dauphin even before she was sixteen.

By 1558 Mary had grown into a very attractive young woman, with bright golden hair, pale creamy skin and dark, almond-shaped eyes. She was about 1.78 m (5 feet 10 inches) tall and carried herself very erect. How different from her future husband! Francis was small for his age, and though he spent most of his time in the fresh air out hunting, he had a sulky face and was never well.

The wedding of Mary and Francis took place on the 24th of April 1558 in the great **cathedral** of Notre Dame in Paris. In the long procession came the Swiss Guards, followed by many musicians, specially dressed in red and yellow, then came one hundred of the King's nobles, followed by the princes and bishops and cardinals (one of

17

This is a drawing of Mary by the artist, Francois Clouet. Can you see why the Queen of France once said, 'Our little Scottish queen has but to smile to turn all French heads'?

them being Mary's uncle). Then came the Dauphin, and last of all Mary, in white with a long train, wearing diamonds at her neck, and a golden crown decked with pearls and rubies and a huge **garnet**. Outside the cathedral they threw gold coins and silver to the people, who made such a noise scrambling for them you could hardly hear the service – we know all this from the account of a Monsieur Briere, who witnessed it all.

Queen of France

Mary's happy, sheltered life was not to last for long. The following year, in June 1559, Francis and she were watching

King Henry taking part in a tournament when he was badly wounded in the head and neck. Within days he was dead. Mary's husband now became King as Francis II, and so Mary was now Queen of France as well as of Scotland.

The men who really ruled France were not members of the royal family, but Mary's uncles, the Duke of Guise and his brother the Cardinal Charles. Francis just enjoyed himself. One day, while he was out hunting, he caught a bad chill. Though doctors did what they could to save him, and Mary nursed him day and night, Francis died shortly afterwards of an infected ear. In December 1560 Mary had already become a widow, and she was only just eighteen.

Though she might have stayed on in France and married again, Mary decided to return to Scotland. Her mother had died in June 1560 leaving the country without a strong ruler. The people had also been fighting over whether Roman Catholicism or Protestantism should be the country's religion. So Mary knew she would have many difficult problems to face. But at least she would be Queen in her own country and not an ex-Queen of France. So, fourteen months later on the morning of the 14th of August 1561, Mary set sail from the port of Calais bound for home.

Things to do

1. Get hold of some books on France and see whether you can find some pictures of castles of this time. They are called châteaux in French. You might get some material from a travel agent if you asked nicely about the châteaux of the Loire. How different is it from England and Scotland at this time? Compare Linlithgow (page 5) and Fontainebleau (page 16).

2. Think about Mary's education. Is it well designed for a princess? Do you think she had an easy or a hard time? Did it turn her into a French princess, or did she stay Scottish at heart, do you think? She always signed her letters 'Marie'.

3 A bad time for the Catholic Church

While Mary was living in France great changes had taken place in Scotland. The religion of the country had been changed from Roman Catholic to Protestant, and England had replaced France as Scotland's ally. The two changes were linked, because in the sixteenth century politics and religion were closely bound up together.

What was wrong with the Church

In the early 1500s, the early sixteenth century, more and more people were finding fault with the Church. Popes and **bishops**, like Cardinal Beaton, spent so much time doing political work that they had little time for their religious duties.

The Church also misused its great wealth. In Scotland the Pope allowed kings to use **monastery** land for rewarding loyal noblemen. As a result monasteries could no longer care for the poor and the sick or even afford to keep up church buildings. Yet when the Church insisted on being paid its taxes it was accused of being greedy.

Little wonder that many priests and other Church people did not do their work properly. **Monks, nuns** and **friars** were said to be lazy, and **parish** priests ignorant and selfish. Instead of setting a good example, many led immoral lives and broke the Church's rules.

Nearly everybody had some grudge against the Church. Kings and nobles were jealous of its power and wealth, while common people resented that it neglected them. Now scholars were saying that much of what the Church taught people to believe was not even true. They said that people should know about the Christian religion straight from the Bible. This meant translating the Bible into modern languages instead of just having it in Latin, which only priests and educated people could read.

The Reformation

What was needed was a thorough clean-up, or **Reformation**, of the Church. It would not be easy. Since it was thought that there was only one way to believe in God, anybody who criticised the Church's teaching could be punished for **heresy** by being burnt to death.

The Reformation started in Germany in 1517 when Martin Luther quarrelled with the Pope and was supported by many of the German princes. Soon they were divided into those who stayed loyal to the Pope, and the others, known as Protestants, who agreed with Luther. In place of the one Catholic Church there grew up many **reformed**, or Protestant, churches, each under its own head, outside of the Roman Catholic Church still under the Pope.

The Reformation comes to Scotland

The ideas of Luther and other reformers spread rapidly to other countries in books and **pamphlets**, now made quickly by the newly-invented printing press. In the reigns of Henry VIII and Edward VI English scholars and priests read about the new ideas about the Church, and the Bible was translated into English for the first time. Many Scots could read English and so these English Bibles were soon smuggled into Scotland.

The ideas of the Reformation were spread also by Protestant preachers. They went about the country saying what was wrong with the Church and how it could be improved according to the ideas of Jesus and his **disciples** in the New Testament. Often these reformers suffered for their beliefs. Patrick Hamilton and George Wishart, for example, were both burnt to death. But the courage they showed often made even more people want to become Protestant.

John Knox

The man who did most to bring about the Reformation in Scotland was a priest from Haddington, called John Knox. Because of his religious beliefs Knox had to live for many years in exile in France, England and Geneva, in Switzerland. In Geneva he met John Calvin, a famous French religious thinker, who had set up a Protestant church which was different from those who followed the ideas of Martin Luther. In Lutheran states the rulers were head of the church and appointed bishops to run it for them. At Geneva the **congregation** ran the church themselves, choosing **elders** who would themselves choose the minister. A church like this is called presbyterian, from 'presbyteros', the Greek word in the New Testament for 'elder'. Knox wanted this kind of church for Scotland.

The Catholic Church tries to reform itself

While Knox was living abroad, leaders of the Catholic Church in Scotland tried to reform it by rooting out some of its worst faults. They agreed that all clergymen should lead better lives and also be better educated. They also printed a **catechism**, written in simple language so that everybody could understand what the Church wanted people to believe. It was written by Archbishop John Hamilton of St Andrews and included parts which were meant to please Protestants. But Hamilton's Catechism came too late to save the Church from being split as nobles and **lairds**, as well as ordinary people, already openly attended Protestant church services.

The Lords of the Congregation

Nobles and lairds became Protestant not only for religious reasons. They thought that Mary of Guise and her French advisers were treating Scotland as if it belonged to France.

This woodcut is believed to be the only true likeness of John Knox (c. 1512–1572). His religious beliefs were based on the Bible, a copy of which is in his hand.

Mary knew that the Church needed to reform itself, but as she depended on its leaders to help her, she had to defend it against the Protestants.

In Edinburgh, on the 10th of December 1557, the Protestant nobles banded themselves together as the **Lords of the Congregation** and said that if necessary they would fight to make Scotland Protestant. They promised:

'before . . . God and his Congregation to . . . maintain, set forward and establish the most blessed word of God and his Congregation . . . and **forsake** and **renounce** the congregation of Satan, with all the superstitions, **abominations** and **idolatry** thereof . . .'

Scotland was becoming divided between Protestants and Catholics, each side believing it was right about religion and the other was wrong.

Things to do

1. Find out more about Martin Luther, John Calvin, Patrick Hamilton and George Wishart. What did each of them do to bring about the Reformation?

2. Find out where the nearest monastery and convent are and what monks, nuns and friars do today.

3. Why do you think some of the important men in Scotland were attracted to the Presbyterian church? Try to give several reasons.

4 Protestant victory

'The rascal multitude'

By 1559 Protestants and Catholics were armed and looking for help from abroad. Remember that at this time Mary Queen of Scots was married to the Dauphin and Mary of Guise could expect more help from France. The Lords of the Congregation hoped for help from England, where the Protestant Elizabeth had become Queen the year before, in 1558, after the death of her Roman Catholic half-sister, Mary.

At Easter Mary of Guise ordered everybody to attend Catholic Church services, and then outlawed Protestants who refused. In May 1559 an angry crowd gathered in St John's Church, Perth, to hear John Knox, newly returned from abroad, preach a powerful **sermon** against the worship of idols in churches. This led to a great outbreak of violence in Perth and other towns by mobs of people – 'the rascal **multitude**' – as Knox called them. In church they knocked down statues of saints, broke stained-glass windows and destroyed anything else to do with the old ways of worship, believing that this was helping to reform the Church.

French and English in Scotland

Only a few weeks after Mary Queen of Scots became Queen of France in July 1559, more French troops landed in Scotland. So the Lords of the Congregation begged the Protestant Elizabeth of England to intervene.

Elizabeth took a long time to make up her mind, not wanting to get involved in helping foreign **rebels**, which is really what the Lords of the Congregation were. But the

French were now saying that as a Protestant Elizabeth had no right to call herself Queen of England, and that the Catholic Mary Queen of Scots was the rightful Queen of England. So, to protect England against the French, Elizabeth finally agreed to help the Scottish Protestants. After centuries of war, Scottish and English soldiers were about to fight on the same side.

The siege of Leith

The English now entered Scotland and began to **besiege** the French by land and sea in their base at Leith. As you can see from the map Leith had strong walls. From these and the church steeples, French gunners fired down on the English as they crept along their trenches to lay mines underneath the walls. But out on the links to the east the English raised large mounds of earth to support their huge cannon. So, from here and from their ships, the English were able to pour blazing shot on to the French in Leith.

After weeks of **bombardment** and hundreds of people dying of disease and starvation, the French saw it was pointless to go on fighting. When Mary of Guise died in June 1560 they asked for a cease-fire and French and English leaders made an agreement known as the Treaty of Edinburgh: each side was to leave Scotland and Mary Queen of Scots would give up calling herself Queen of England.

The Treaty of Edinburgh ended the Auld Alliance between Scotland and France. While France remained Roman Catholic, Scotland now became friendlier with England, the Auld Enemy, both being Protestant countries.

The New Kirk

The French and English said nothing about religion in the Treaty of Edinburgh, wisely leaving the Scots to decide this for themselves. In August 1560 the Scottish Parliament met in Edinburgh and passed laws making Scotland a Protestant

This map shows Edinburgh with its castle in the background and Leith with its defences in the centre foreground. The lines surrounding the port are the trenches of the English attackers.

country. These ended the rule of the Pope over the Church in Scotland, and made illegal the saying of **mass**.

Parliament also approved the Confession of Faith which listed the beliefs of the new Protestant Church. It was written by John Knox, now minister of St Giles, the high **kirk** of Edinburgh. Knox wrote also the Book of Discipline, in which he set out his plans for how the Kirk should be run. These were based on the ideas of John Calvin, whom you read about in Chapter 3. The Church of Scotland was therefore to be a **presbyterian** church with a minister in each parish chosen by the congregation and having elected elders and **deacons** to help him. Ministers, elders and deacons formed the **kirk session** to carry out the Kirk's laws in the parish. Representatives of all the kirk sessions would meet to pass laws for the whole of the Church of Scotland in annual meetings of the General Assembly under an elected **moderator**. Unlike priests in the Roman Catholic Church, ministers of the Kirk could get married.

All church members, as well as ministers, were to be well educated. Since everybody had to be able to read the Bible, children had to go to school. So, there was to be a school in every parish, with the minister hearing the catechism to test children's religious knowledge.

How was the Kirk to pay for education as well as caring for the poor and the sick, building churches and giving ministers and their families a proper **stipend**? The Book of Discipline had the answer: out of money from the valuable lands of the old Roman Catholic Church. But much of the Church's landed wealth was already in the hands of the government and of the nobles and lairds, many of whom were Protestant and unlikely to give it up willingly. So, though many of the ideas in the Book of Discipline were very sensible, they were not easy to carry out. This was only one of the many difficult problems facing Mary Queen of Scots when she came back to Scotland in 1561.

Things to do

1. Make a list of the ways in which the Scottish Reformation was to do with religion and another list to show what it was to do with politics.

2. Think about Elizabeth's problem about interfering in Scotland in 1560. Make a list of reasons in favour of interference, and one against. Was she wise in choosing to go in, do you think?

3. Find out as much as you can about the organisation and work of the Church of Scotland today. How is it similar to and different from the Church set up in the time of John Knox?

5 Mary's reign in Scotland: the happy years

Welcome home

A heavy haar, or cold mist, hung over the Firth of Forth that August day in 1561 when Mary's ships brought her into Leith. But her subjects gave her a warm enough welcome and followed her all the way to the Palace of Holyroodhouse, her main Scottish home.

There was a ceremonial entry into Edinburgh, and then after three weeks at the palace, Mary went on a short tour

In this drawing made during 'the rough wooing' you can see close up the Palace of Holyroodhouse, Mary's Edinburgh home. Notice how close the palace is to the town. In what ways might this have been a disadvantage to Mary?

Scotland at the time
of Queen Mary.

Castles
Abbeys and Priories
Battles

0   100 km

ORKNEY

Aberdeen

ANGUS

Perth
Falkland
Inchmahome   Lochleven   St Andrews
Stirling   Dysart   FIFE
Falkirk   Queensferry
Dumbarton   LENNOX   Leith   Haddington
Glasgow   Linlithgow   Dunbar
Langside   Edinburgh   Pinkie
Craigmillar   Carberry Hill
Kelso   Berwick
Melrose   Dryburgh
R.Tweed   Jedburgh

Hermitage

Dumfries
Solway Moss
Carlisle

of her kingdom. She visited her birth-place at Linlithgow, Stirling (where she had been kept safe from English invaders), and then on to Dundee and St Andrews. Every-where happy crowds came out to see their beautiful young Queen, who was not yet twenty.

Warm though their welcome was, Mary must have found Scotland cold and bleak compared with France; and how bare and gloomy her palaces and castles would be in contrast to those she knew in France. But she did her best to make them comfortable with the fine tapestries, warm beds and soft cushions she had brought with her.

Soon she settled down to the kind of life she had led in France. In her leisure hours she went **hawking** and hunting in the woods around Falkland Palace, and at Stir-ling she practised archery. Down on the sands at Seton in East Lothian she learned to play the Scottish game of golf.

When it was too wet or cold to go out she would stay indoors and play chess, cards or backgammon. In the evenings she and her courtiers would entertain themselves, singing part-songs, playing on their lutes and taking part in fancy-dress parties. For company she always had those childhood friends, her 'Four Maries', with whom she spent many a happy hour, chatting away and listening to their gossip, while doing her needlework, her favourite pastime.

Mary's advisers

The English **ambassador** reported that Mary often did her sewing at meetings of her Privy Council, those men she chose to help her to govern the country. Mary's two chief advisers were both very able men, Lord James Stewart and Sir William Maitland of Lethington. Lord James was her half-brother, an **illegitimate** son of James V. He had been one of those Lords of the Congregation who brought about the Scottish Reformation, and he was determined to keep Scotland Protestant. Lethington was her Secretary of State and he attended to all the day-to-day business of govern-ment. He, too, was a Protestant, but was less interested in religion. His main aim was to improve relations between Scotland and England so that one day they might be united under Mary as Queen.

Thanks to Lethington and Lord James, Scotland became more peaceful. They restored order in the Borders where people had almost given up obeying the law altogether. Members of families, such as the Kerrs, the Scotts, the Humes and the Elliots, were for ever fighting among themselves or with English Border families. Now some of them were brought to trial and put to death. The Borders had never been so law-abiding as they were under Mary.

Mary and John Knox

Like many rulers in the sixteenth century, the most pressing problems that Mary had to deal with were to do with religion. Though Scotland was now a Protestant country, Mary was a Roman Catholic and intended to remain so. Of course, she would have liked all her subjects to be Catholic too, but she knew that this was now impossible. So, she issued a **proclamation** soon after her return, saying that there were to be no more changes in religion for the time being, but that she and her courtiers were to be allowed to worship as Catholics.

This arrangement pleased most people, including Lethington and Lord James. But extreme Protestants, like John Knox, distrusted Mary. From his pulpit in St Giles', the high kirk of Edinburgh, Knox spoke out fiercely against Catholic services being held at court and he was not above denouncing the Queen herself. In one of his sermons he declared:

'Princes are more exercised in fidelling and **fliging** than in reading or hearing of God's most blessed Word. . . . Musicians and flatterers, these corrupters of youth, please them better than do men old and wise who desire, with their **salutary exhortations**, to tame some of that pride which is our common circle and sinful heritage.'

Mary and he met four times but they could never agree. Knox was sure that Mary was plotting with the Pope and other Catholic rulers to make Scotland Catholic again, while she looked on him as a very bold, outspoken and unruly subject.

In fact, Mary helped the Kirk more than Knox would admit. For example, she turned down offers from the Catholic Earl of Huntly to help to make the country Catholic again by force. And though she often told the Pope how loyal a Catholic she was, she did very little to bring the Catholic religion back again.

Mary also helped the Kirk in a practical way. She saw she could not take away from the lairds and nobles their Church lands, which amounted to about two-thirds of the wealth of the old Church. But she handed over to the Kirk part of the rest, so that ministers could get their stipends and the work of the Kirk could continue. It provided much less money than the Kirk needed, but it was probably the best arrangement possible at the time.

Altogether then, the first four years of Mary's reign were successful, all things considered. With the help of Lethington and Lord James, she had restored order again and had avoided upsetting either her Catholic subjects or the new Kirk. Apart from those who wanted to force the Catholic religion on Scotland, and those like John Knox who thought she should turn Protestant, most of Mary's subjects were fairly content with what she was doing.

Mary and Elizabeth of England

To be completely successful as a ruler Mary had also to get on well with her neighbour, Elizabeth of England. The two Queens often wrote to each other and exchanged gifts but they never met.

Elizabeth always kept a wary eye on events in Scotland, especially since Mary had never signed the Treaty of Edinburgh, which you read about in the last chapter. Like other Roman Catholics, Mary believed that Elizabeth was

The Armes of mary Queene Dolphines of Fran
Tho noblest Lady on Earth far, till aduance
Of Scotland. Queene. & of England also.
Of Ireland, als. God hath prouiditt. so.

illegitimate with no right to be Queen because her parents had not been properly married. As Mary was her nearest Catholic relative, Catholics looked on her as the rightful Queen of England. Mary's advisers tried to persuade her to sign the Treaty. Only after a lot of talk did Mary say she would sign, but only if Elizabeth agreed to name her as her **heir**. Elizabeth did not want to say who should succeed her, however, in case Catholics tried to kill her and make Mary Queen in her place. So Mary never signed the Treaty of Edinburgh and kept up her claim to the English throne. As a result the two Queens could not become friends.

Enter Lord Darnley

Unlike Elizabeth, who remained single, Mary had already been married and wanted to marry again. But whom was she to marry? It was important that she made a wise choice because her husband would rule Scotland alongside her as King. She could not marry one of her own nobles in case the others became jealous. But if she married a foreign prince she would make enemies abroad as well as at home: a Protestant husband would offend Catholics and a Catholic would displease Elizabeth and other Protestants. No matter whom she married, it seemed that Mary was sure to upset someone.

Elizabeth took a great interest in all Mary's marriage plans. It was she who sent to Scotland the young Lord Darnley, son of the Earl of Lennox, a Scottish nobleman who had been forced to leave his country some years before. Even before his arrival early in 1565 people had said that he might be a suitable husband for Mary. As you can see from the family tree on page 8, Mary and he were cousins, both having the same grandmother, Margaret

This is a portrait by an unknown artist of Mary's second husband, Henry, Lord Darnley (c. 1546–1567) when he was about twenty. The artist has tried to make Darnley look his best, so what does the picture tell us about the idea of good looks and fashion for men at this time? What does the portrait also tell you about Darnley's character?

Tudor. Though brought up as a Catholic he had attended Protestant services. So people thought he might please both Protestants and Catholics.

Mary had met Darnley before in France. Now he was nearly nineteen and was very handsome looking. He was about 1.83 m (6 feet) tall, which suited Mary because she was very tall too. Altogether he seemed to be an ideal husband. Soon Mary had fallen headlong in love with him and asked him to marry her.

Nobody else, however, wanted Mary to marry Lord Darnley. Her half-brother, Lord James – now known as the Earl of Moray – disliked him, partly because he would now take his place as the Queen's chief adviser. Lethington was against the marriage because it could upset Queen Elizabeth who did not want to see Mary married to another close heir to the English throne. And as for John Knox, he was afraid that with a Catholic husband Mary would now openly try to make Scotland Catholic too. But Mary was still determined to marry Darnley whatever they said. So the wedding took place in Holyrood Abbey on Sunday, 29th July 1565. As Lethington had guessed, Elizabeth was furious. Mary replied:

'I am truly amazed at my good sister's dissatisfaction, for the choice which she now blames was made in accordance with her wishes. I have rejected all foreign suitors and have chosen an Englishman who is of the royal blood of both kingdoms, and, as far as England is concerned, is on his mother's side, the eldest male descendant from the royal house of Tudor.'

Things to do

1. Some people say of Mary at this time that she was idle and just pleased herself rather than taking control of government. Others would say she did the best that anyone could do in the circumstances. Prepare a list of arguments for both cases and then see what you think.

2. Why are kings and queens not supposed to choose their partners in marriage on the grounds of love alone? Do you think Mary was wrong to marry Darnley because she thought she was in love with him?

6 Mary's reign in Scotland: the unhappy years

The Chaseabout Raid

At first Mary's marriage made her very happy. Darnley and she seemed to be well-matched. To show how much she trusted him she announced that he was to be known as King Henry so that either of them could sign official papers. But the nobles could not stand their new king because he was so conceited. The Earl of Moray had no time for him at all. A few days after the wedding he rallied his men at Ayr and marched on Edinburgh, claiming that Mary was trying to make Scotland Catholic again.

Mary acted cooly and swiftly. With Darnley at her side to boost her confidence, she joined her army which had **mustered** at Falkirk and Stirling. When Moray entered Edinburgh he found nobody to support him. Hearing that Mary was returning with an army five times bigger than his, he retreated to Dumfries. There he waited for the help that Elizabeth of England had promised to send him.

But no help came. Elizabeth never liked to be seen giving help to rebels, especially unsuccessful ones like Moray. So, when Mary and her army drew near he fled across the border. Since Mary had chased her enemies out of Scotland, this rebellion in September 1565 is known as the Chaseabout Raid.

'Seigneur Davie'

You can imagine how proud Mary felt. With her husband to help her she had overcome powerful enemies. By early November she had become even more confident when she knew she was expecting a baby the following June. Soon she would have an heir to rule Scotland after her.

But Mary had a new friend. He was an Italian, David Riccio, who had come to Scotland in 1561 as a servant of the ambassador of the Duke of Savoy. Since he was a fine singer he was invited to join Mary's group of court musicians. By 1564 he had become one of her private secretaries and dealt with a lot of secret government business. He became so powerful that if anyone wanted to speak to the Queen they had first to ask him.

Riccio was a small man of humble birth, but so full of his own importance that courtiers sneeringly called him '**Seigneur** Davie'. Nobles hated him because he was a foreigner as well as a commoner. John Knox was sure that he was a secret agent of the Pope, sent to bring down the Protestant religion.

Murder at Holyrood

Mary's enemies saw how they could use Riccio in their plots against her, especially when it became known that her marriage had broken down. After only a few months Mary had discovered what a weak and foolish husband Darnley was. Instead of helping her to govern the country, he preferred to go out hunting and drinking and to pass the time with other women. Then he sulked because Mary would not let him be crowned king.

Enemies of Mary – friends of Moray – now told Darnley that the Queen and Riccio were lovers. As expected, Darnley was foolish enough to believe them and became so jealous of Riccio that he joined in a deadly plot, signing a **bond** with other Scottish lords, by which they agreed to kill Riccio and crown Darnley king in Mary's place. An English diplomat, who supported the plot wrote to Elizabeth on February 18th 1566:

'I now know for certain that the Queen regrets her marriage, and hates her husband and all his **kin**. I know also that he believes he will have a **partake** in his play and game, and that certain **intrigues** have been going on between father and son to seize the crown against her will. I know that if these come to fruition David, with the King's assent, will have his throat cut within the next ten days.'

On Saturday, the 9th of March 1566, the plotters secretly surrounded the Palace of Holyroodhouse. Upstairs in a small candle-lit room, the Queen was having supper as usual with a few close friends, including Riccio. Unexpectedly, Darnley joined them. A quarrel started in which Darnley accused Mary of being unfaithful. Suddenly noises could be heard in the private stairway outside. The door then burst open and there in the doorway stood one of the **conspirators**, Lord Ruthven, a suit of armour showing under his cloak. When he demanded that the Queen hand over Riccio, Mary refused and ordered Ruthven to leave. Other conspirators then swarmed into the room. They made for Riccio, who cowered behind the Queen, clinging to her skirts in frantic terror. Grabbing Darnley's dagger, one of the plotters lunged forward and buried it in Riccio's side. Then all was confusion. Chairs and tables were overturned and candles swept away. There were screams and ugly shouts. Someone brought a light. There in the candle-glow stood the Queen, six months pregnant, with one of the plotters pointing a pistol at her stomach, helpless while the wounded Riccio, kicking and shrieking for mercy, was dragged outside and hacked to death. Later, more than fifty wounds were counted on the little Italian's body, which lay bleeding where it had been thrown at the foot of the stairs. The conspirators left Darnley's dagger in the body.

The Earl of Bothwell

Afterwards when Mary was told that Riccio was dead, she is reported to have said, 'No more tears; I will think upon a revenge.' In the meantime she was powerless, a prisoner in her own palace, her husband on the side of her enemies. Over 120 people had been involved in the plot.

But Mary was patient. Within a few days she had won over Darnley. He said he had only been involved with planning the return of the Protestant lords to Scotland: he had nothing to do with the murder and agreed to try to escape from the palace with her. With the help of some loyal guards they managed to slip out of the palace one night and rode off eastwards down the coast to the castle of Dunbar. There they were joined by some faithful nobles. A few days later Mary rode back to Edinburgh with an army of 8,000 men while her enemies fled back to England.

Mary then followed up her victory by turning her enemies against each other. She ordered the murderers of Riccio to be brought to trial, but forgave her half-brother for his part in the Chaseabout Raid and even took him back into the government. But she could never forgive Darnley. He had tried to kill not only Riccio but herself and their unborn child. Till then she had only despised her husband but now she loathed him.

Not even the birth of their baby son in Edinburgh Castle in June 1566 could bring Mary and Darnley together. He still treated her badly and neglected his duties as king. By October Mary had become ill and low-spirited. She turned for help and advice to one of her loyal nobles. This was James Hepburn, Earl of Bothwell, one of the most powerful men in Scotland, with lands scattered over the southern counties. He prided himself on his loyalty to the royal family. Most Scottish nobles took bribes from England but he took none.

Bothwell was just over thirty, about 1.6 m (5 feet 3 inches) tall and with a dark complexion. Because he was not very tall someone described him as looking like 'an ape in purple'. Many women, however, found him very attractive, though men distrusted him because he was so ambitious. Many feared that he was out for nothing less than control of Scotland.

With a weak fool for a husband, Mary valued Bothwell for his loyalty and strength. So much did he mean to her

Mary's third husband, James Hepburn, Earl of Bothwell (c. 1535–1578). From this portrait by an unknown artist in 1566, can you see that he had led a rough life and that few people could trust him?

that when he lay wounded in his Border castle at Hermitage in October 1566, she rode about 30 km (50 miles) over rough country in one day just to see him. Already, some people said, Mary was secretly in love with him. But this was not necessarily so. She may have been interested in him only as a useful friend and adviser.

The Kirk o' Field mystery

Whatever her feelings for Bothwell, Mary made no secret of her wish to be rid of Darnley. But how was it to be done? If she were to divorce him she might make her son illegitimate and so prevent him from becoming king after her. In November at Craigmillar Castle, near Edinburgh, Bothwell and some of her other nobles offered her a way out of her difficulties. They promised to help her, assuring her that she would 'see nothing but good' from their plans, whatever they were.

At the end of the year Mary and her courtiers gathered at Stirling Castle for the christening of little Prince James. Darnley played little part in the celebrations, not even turning up for the actual christening. Just after Christmas he left Stirling and went to Glasgow, near his father's lands in the Lennox district. On the way it was reported that 'he fell deadly sick' of an infectious disease referred to as 'the pox'. About a month later Mary went to see him. Was she really sorry for him, or was she just making sure that he was not plotting against her again? Whatever the reason for her visit, she brought him back to Edinburgh with her once he was feeling better.

Darnley chose to live in an old house, known as Kirk o' Field, which stood not far from the Palace just outside the city wall. Mary often went to see him and twice spent the night there. She intended to sleep at Kirk o' Field once again on Sunday, the 9th of February 1567, the night before Darnley was due to come home. At the last moment, however, Mary suddenly remembered she had promised to attend the wedding of one of her courtiers, and so at about ten o'clock she returned to the palace.

Early the next morning, at two o'clock, the people of Edinburgh were wakened by a terrible explosion. Kirk o' Field had been blown up! In the garden of the house lay the naked body of Darnley, with the corpse of his manservant nearby. No trace of the explosion could be found on either of the bodies, but both men had been strangled. Look at the sketch on page 44 which shows the events of the Kirk o' Field murder.

Marriage to Bothwell

Darnley had many enemies, including the murderers of Riccio who had never forgiven him for betraying them to the Queen. But the one whom everyone blamed for his murder was the man who seemed to gain the most from Darnley's death, Mary's right-hand man, the Earl of Bothwell. He had been in town at the time and was known to

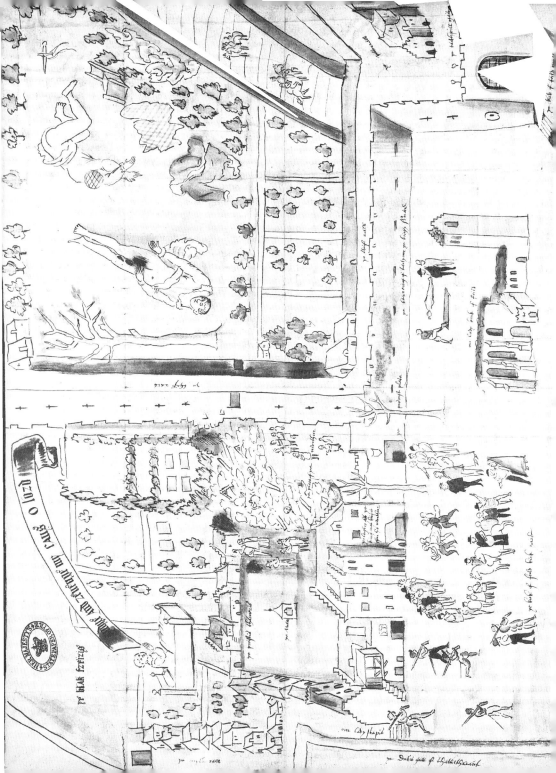

Opposite: Study this sketch made for Queen Elizabeth of the scene at Kirk o' Field after Darnley's murder. It shows events that happened at different times. You will be able to see the remains of the house beside the city wall. Can you pick out the bodies of Darnley and his servant, as well as a dagger, a chair and Darnley's dressing-gown? In the top left corner Darnley's and Mary's son is shown in his cot with the words 'Judge and Avenge My Cause, O Lord'. This is meant to be a propaganda picture. Can you think what the message is?

be ruthless enough to kill anyone who stood in his way. It was even said that the Queen herself might have been involved in the murder because her feelings for him were well known. So, when she promoted him to an important position in the government, they said that Bothwell and she must have planned the murder together. Whether or not she was involved, Mary now made mistake after mistake. She made no attempt to bring Bothwell to trial: this was left to Darnley's father, the Earl of Lennox. And when the trial took place, Edinburgh was so full of Bothwell's men that the jury were too scared to find him guilty.

One startling event followed another in that year, 1567. About the end of April the Queen was on her way back from visiting her little son at Stirling when she was waylaid by Bothwell and his men and carried off to his castle at Dunbar. Was Mary really forced to go or had she and Bothwell planned this as a way of getting Mary into Bothwell's power? Again no one knows. What we do know is that when she later got the chance to escape she did not take it. At the time, however, people felt that Mary did want to be captured by Bothwell.

They were not surprised, then, when Bothwell was speedily divorced by his wife and within less than a month married to Mary at Holyrood. Why did Mary marry Bothwell? Was it out of love or was she forced? Or did she marry him just to make sure of his support against her enemies? Once again historians cannot agree. One thing is certain, Mary's third marriage brought her no happiness. By marrying the man who was strongly suspected of murdering Lord Darnley, Mary threw away any chance of making a success of her reign. Since Bothwell was a

Protestant and the marriage was carried out by a Protestant minister, even the Pope would have nothing more to do with her.

Partly out of jealousy of Bothwell, Mary became more and more isolated and bewildered. Another group of nobles, led by the Earl of Argyll, now raised an army and said that they wanted to free her from his control and to avenge the death of Darnley. They called themselves the 'confederate lords'. Mary and Bothwell rode out from Dunbar to meet them with their much smaller army. The two armies faced each other near Musselburgh at Carberry Hill in June 1567. But there was no fighting. Mary's men simply drifted away. While Bothwell rode off, saying he was going to raise another army (in fact he deserted her, in return for being allowed to go free on promise of the Queen's safety), Mary gave herself up to her enemies. This was the last that Mary and Bothwell were ever to see of each other. Now deserted and humiliated, Mary was led back as a prisoner to Edinburgh and put up at a house in the High Street. Where they once used to cheer her the crowds now mocked her and called her the most terrible names.

Lochleven

The next day Mary was taken down to Leith, ferried across to Fife and imprisoned in a castle on an island in Lochleven. For the next fortnight she was so exhausted she could hardly eat or drink. In July, she had a miscarriage of twins.

Meanwhile, the victorious nobles had to decide what to do with their Queen. Since she refused to divorce Bothwell, they finally forced her to give up her throne. They made her baby son King in her place as James VI, with the Earl of Moray as Regent. At the end of July the little King, aged thirteen months, was solemnly crowned in the Church of the Holy **Rude** in Stirling, with John Knox preaching the sermon.

Now that she had abdicated, Mary might have expected

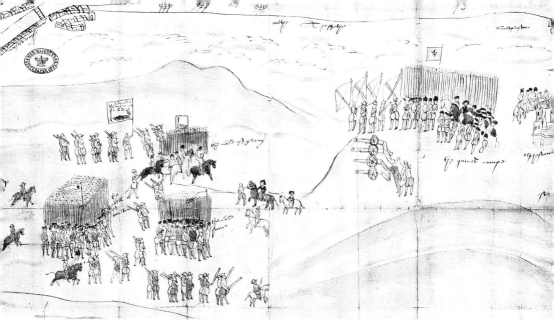

An unknown artist drew this sketch at Carberry Hill in June 1567. The rebel lords with their three squadrons of troops are on the left. The Queen's army, flying Scottish flags and the royal standard, is on the right. Which army seems to be the larger? Which appears to be the stronger? In the centre of the picture you can see Mary being led over to the rebel lords.

to receive more freedom. Instead, she was watched over more closely than ever in case someone tried to free her. But there seemed little chance of that because Mary's friends were too frightened of Moray. As for Bothwell, having failed to raise another army, he had fled to Orkney and Shetland and finally ended up as a prisoner in Denmark.

Within the Castle of Lochleven, however, a friend was planning Mary's escape. This was George Douglas, the brother of her jailer. His first attempt failed, because while being rowed across the loch dressed as a washerwoman, Mary gave herself away with her smooth, pale hands.

Douglas's second attempt did succeed. Mary had also won over a young page in the castle, named Willie Douglas. On Sunday, the 2nd of May 1568, while serving his master's supper, he picked up the castle keys with his napkin. Eagerly waiting were the Queen and her maid-servant, dressed as countrywomen. All three casually walked out of the castle, locked the gates behind them and dropped the keys into a cannon. A boat was waiting. With the Queen tucked under the seat, Willie Douglas rowed the boat ashore. There, George Douglas was waiting with horses. Accompanied by Willie Douglas, Mary rode off. Two miles on they were joined by Lord Seton, one of her most devoted followers, who took her across the Forth to his castle at Niddry, not far from Queensferry. After ten months a prisoner Mary slept her first night in freedom again.

Langside

Next morning she was off again riding fast to the west, where members of the powerful Hamilton family were ready to help her. Within a few days more than thirty very influential people had promised to help her with an army of more than 5,000 men, which shows how popular Mary still was.

At the head of this army Mary now made for Dumbarton Castle, which she intended to use as her base for winning back her kingdom. At Glasgow, however, the Regent Moray barred her way with his army. On the 13th of May the two armies met south of Glasgow at the village of Lang-side. Though the Queen had more men than the Regent, they were very badly led. So, from a nearby hill, Mary had to watch her men being mown down and scattered. Though she had to be held back from riding down and rallying on her men herself, she was finally persuaded to flee for safety.

Over wild and trackless country Mary now rode south-wards to Dumfries where she hoped for support from some of her Catholic nobles and lairds. She wrote, later, in a letter to her uncle Charles, the Cardinal of Lorraine:

'I have suffered injuries, **calumnies**, captivity, hunger, cold, heat, flying – without knowing to whither – four score and twelve miles across the country, without once pausing to alight, and then lay on the hard ground, having only sour milk to drink, and oatmeal to eat, without bread, passing three nights like the owls.'

Now Mary had to make up her mind what to do next. Finally she decided there was only one thing she could do, to leave Scotland and go to England. Elizabeth had been her enemy, it is true, but perhaps by meeting her, Mary might persuade her cousin to help her to regain her throne. At three o'clock in the afternoon on Sunday, the 16th of May 1568, she sailed out across the Solway Firth in a small fishing boat. Four hours later she was in England. Mary had been in Scotland for less than seven years.

Things to do

1. Mary's judgement of people seems poor, especially when it comes to men. But was she to blame in this entirely? Think about what she said to Darnley when she showed him their baby for the first time:

   'My lord, here I protest to God, and as I shall answer to Him at the great day of judgement, this is your son, and no other man's son; and I am desirous that all here, both ladies and others, bear witness for he is so much your son that I fear it may be the worse for him hereafter.'

   What did she mean by 'may be the worse for him hereafter'?

2. If you were investigating the case of the Darnley murder, what theories might you explore? What evidence would seem important to you? What other evidence would you seek?

3. Bothwell was no handsome man, and ended his days stark mad. Why should Mary have put herself in his power? Again, do you think she was quite to blame?

4. Whatever made her think of England as a place to seek help? Was there anything else she could have done?

7 Prisoner in England

Unwelcome guest

Mary's sudden arrival in England took everybody by surprise. It was the last thing Elizabeth expected or wanted. Mary was taken to the castle at Carlisle, where the warden treated her with great respect, but wondered what to do with her. Elizabeth did not know either. She would probably have liked to send her back to Scotland but was afraid of upsetting her ally, the Protestant Regent Moray. If she allowed her to stay, English Catholics might try to make her queen in place of Elizabeth. Elizabeth's advisers were quite sure that the sooner Mary was safely locked up the better. So she was taken to Bolton castle in the wilds of North Yorkshire, far away from the Scottish border.

The Casket Letters

The English government now had time to decide what to do next. They set up a **commission** to look into Mary's quarrel with her nobles. It met at York and heard arguments from both sides. Before long the enquiry turned into a kind of trial, with Mary having to defend herself against Moray and his friends.

During the enquiry Moray's men produced a mysterious silver **casket**, which they said had been taken from one of Bothwell's servants. It contained a collection of papers, including some love letters which appeared to have been written between Mary and Bothwell before the death of Darnley. These Casket Letters, as they are called, were meant to prove that Mary and Bothwell had planned Darnley's murder.

For centuries people have argued whether or not the Casket Letters were genuine. Nowadays many think that they were false and made up of parts of letters written by Mary and Bothwell to other people. If so we shall never know who made them up because the original letters disappeared a long time ago: we have only copies of the letters, which makes it impossible to check the original handwriting. At the time, Elizabeth and her advisers did not think the letters were very important. So the enquiry was closed with neither side satisfied. But Mary remained in England, held prisoner not because of any crime she had committed but because Elizabeth could not think of anything else to do with her.

Elizabeth's prisoner

Thus began Mary's long years of captivity, spent in various English castles. From Bolton she was moved early in 1569 to Tutbury in Staffordshire. It was a bleak place, nearly in ruins and overlooking a marsh. The dampness gave Mary terrible colds and rheumatism. Her jailer was the Earl of Shrewsbury, a fussy but kindly sort of man, who was dominated by his wife, Elizabeth, known as Bess of Hardwick. You can read more about her in the 'Then and There' book *The Elizabethan Country House*.

On the whole Mary was not treated badly in prison. At first she was allowed to have visitors, although they were carefully watched in case they tried to help her to escape. She had her own courtiers for company as well as servants. These included the faithful George and Willie Douglas from Lochleven, as well as her dear old friend, Mary Seton, the only one of her 'Four Maries' who did not get married. All of them were paid out of money that she got from her lands in France.

Mary passed her days in prison as best she could. Tirelessly she embroidered cushion-covers, tapestries and bed hangings. For exercise she was allowed to go out hunting. She was even allowed to go to the mineral water baths at

This is part of a piece of embroidery sewn by Mary while she was a prisoner in England. It is a monogram of her name in French. See if you can disentangle the letters to form MARIE STUART. (The 'U' is shown as a 'V').

Buxton for the sake of her health. She looked forward to these visits to town because she was able to meet people. Then Elizabeth got to hear of it and the outings were stopped. Mary wrote many letters to friends and rulers of other countries, but these had often to be smuggled out to avoid the prying eyes of her jailers. She wrote letters to Elizabeth, begging to be released or at least to see her, but Elizabeth always said no.

Catholic plots

Many Catholics in England hoped to free Mary and replace Elizabeth. For help they turned to Philip II, the powerful Roman Catholic ruler of Spain. They also involved the Pope in their schemes. In 1570 he **excommunicated** Elizabeth, which meant that Roman Catholics need no longer obey her.

By the 1580s Catholics and Protestants were at each other's throats all over Europe. Laws were made against Catholics in England. In Paris a terrible **massacre** of Protestants had taken place in 1572. In the Netherlands the Protestant Dutch under William the Silent, Prince of Orange, rose in revolt against Philip of Spain. Soldiers from England went to help the Dutch. At sea, English sailors raided Spanish treasure ships carrying gold and silver from mines in America. War between Protestant England and Catholic Spain seemed unavoidable.

In 1584 a Catholic murdered William the Silent. People in England were scared that someone might murder Queen Elizabeth, that their country would be torn by civil war and invaded by Spanish troops. The hated mass would be said in English churches and Mary made Queen of England. Now more than ever before, Protestant English people looked on Mary with fear and hatred.

The man who made it his business to stamp out any Catholic plots was Elizabeth's Secretary of State, Sir Francis Walsingham. An Act of Parliament was passed which said that anyone who plotted to kill the Queen or who gained from such a plot should be put to death. Though he knew that Mary must be involved in plots against Elizabeth he did not have enough evidence to prove her guilty. Now he used his many spies to lure Mary into a deadly trap.

A trap to catch a Queen

Mary had now been Elizabeth's prisoner for seventeen years. At the end of 1585 she was moved from Tutbury Castle to the moated manor house of Chartley nearby. Now

Mary's royal jailer, Elizabeth of England, shown here in all her finery by an unknown artist about 1575. This, too, is a propaganda picture. Can you tell what it is saying about the Queen?

she was in the care of Sir Amyas Paulet, a harsh, cruel man who disliked her intensely. He did everything possible to make life unpleasant for her, even forbidding her to go out for exercise. He also stopped her from receiving any letters, which made Mary feel cut off from the outside world and desperate to know what was going on.

Walsingham persuaded one of Mary's secret agents, Gilbert Gifford, to become one of his spies and act as a 'double' agent. This was their plan: Gifford was to get Mary to start writing letters again to the French ambassador in London; Walsingham would allow the ambassador to pass on letters between Mary and her friends in France; and Gifford was to make sure that all Mary's letters were opened and read.

Gifford had also to arrange for Mary's letters to be smuggled out and in. He used the casks used for beer made in the local town of Burton-upon-Trent. Mary leapt at the chance of getting in touch with her friends again. She wrote her letters, which her secretary put into code, and then wrapped them up in a leather case that was stuffed into the stopper of an empty beer-cask. The brewer took away the empty barrels and handed the packet of letters to Gifford who was supposed to deliver them to the French ambassador. Unknown to Mary, however, Gifford first passed on the letters to Walsingham and his agents who had broken her code. So Mary's enemies knew all about what passed in her secret letters.

Among the people who wrote to Mary was Sir Anthony Babington, a rich young Catholic gentleman from Derbyshire, who planned to free her. Walsingham now arranged for Babington and Mary to write more letters to each other. Soon he knew all about Babington's plot. Elizabeth was to be murdered, Mary set free, and with foreign help made Queen of England.

By the end of 1586, Walsingham had enough evidence of Mary's guilt. All he had to do was to round up Babington and the other conspirators. Mary knew nothing of all this when one day in August her jailer suddenly said that she could go out hunting. When she saw some horsemen riding across the moors to meet her she thought they might be friends coming to rescue her. But instead they had been sent to arrest her. Mary had fallen right into Walsingham's trap.

This is the last portrait painted of Mary while she was still alive. It was painted in 1578 by Nicholas Hilliard. How old was she then?

Trial and execution

Mary was taken to Fotheringay, a tall grim castle that seemed to frown over the flat Northamptonshire countryside. Meanwhile, a group of thirty-six lords and judges prepared to bring her to trial. At first Mary refused to have anything to do with such proceedings, saying that no court had the right to try a queen. Finally, however, she agreed to appear and defend herself against their charges.

Mary's trial took place in a long room above the great hall of the castle. It lasted two days. It was just after nine o'clock in the morning of the 14th of October 1586 when the trial began. The noise and chatter of the large crowd of judges and spectators died down when Mary entered and took her seat. Instead of the dazzling young woman of whom poets had sung, people now saw a limping, middle-aged woman, with a pale, puffy face, her body bent with rheumatism and plump from lack of exercise. She looked around her and said: 'How many lawyers are here assembled and not one of them to represent me.'

Yet throughout her trial everybody was struck by the dignified way she behaved. Mary denied all the charges of plotting against Queen Elizabeth; anything she had done was simply to free herself from unlawful imprisonment. As was usual at this time in criminal cases, Mary had to conduct her own defence without any help from lawyers. She knew no English law and was not allowed to see any of the documents brought in evidence against her.

At the end of the trial the judges rode off to speak to Queen Elizabeth in London. No one was surprised when they found Mary guilty. It was now up to Elizabeth to pass sentence of death. But for nearly three months Elizabeth put off signing the death warrant. Though she knew that as long as Mary lived she was not safe, she hated the idea of putting another queen to death. All the while her advisers urged her to sign. Both Houses of Parliament added their voice in an address to the Queen:

> 'We cannot find that there is any possible means to provide for your Majesty's safety but by the fast and speedy execution of the said Queen.'

But Elizabeth hesitated:

> '. . . I must **avow** it hath always been my innermost wish to find some other way of achieving your safety and mine own welfare than the one that is proposed . . . Since, however, it hath now been determined that my safety cannot be secured in any other way than by her death I am profoundly mournful that I, . . . should be compelled to show cruelty to such a highly placed princess . . . I beg you to excuse my inward doubts, and not to take it amiss that I send you an answer which is no answer.'

At the same time foreign rulers begged her to show mercy. From Scotland came a feeble protest from James VI, Mary's son, now aged nearly twenty. But Elizabeth

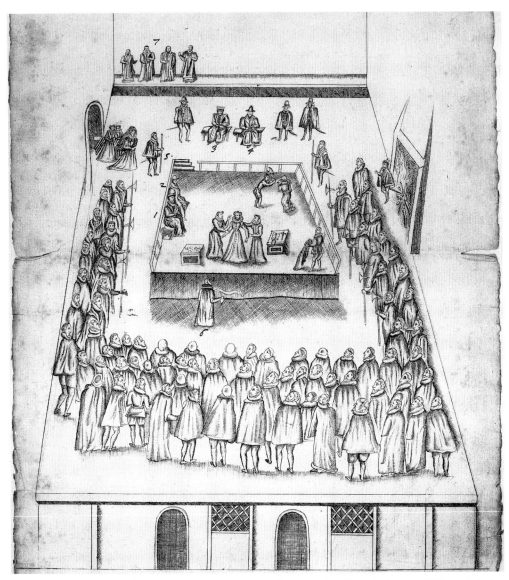

An unknown spectator at Fotheringay Castle in February 1587 sketched this scene of Mary's execution. Look for Mary, shown three times: firstly, being led in with her ladies (top left), then facing a crowd of onlookers as she prepares for her execution, and finally, kneeling down with her head on the block. For whom might this drawing have been made?

knew she need not take his protest seriously: when she died he had a good claim to her throne and so James dared not offend Elizabeth in case she did not name him as her successor. Besides, James had never known his mother, and his guardians had brought him up to hate her.

In January 1587 Elizabeth could put off signing Mary's death warrant no longer. Alarming stories were going about of another plot to kill her, of Mary having escaped, of London being on fire, and of Spanish troops having landed in Wales. Finally, it is said, her secretary placed Mary's death warrant under a pile of papers on her table, and so without looking, Elizabeth signed away Mary's life.

Mary spent her last days quietly. In these later years her religion had been a great comfort, so she prayed for much of the time. On the day fixed for her execution, Wednesday the 8th of February 1587, she rose early and dressed in her best gown of black satin. Calmly she went downstairs to the great hall where a large crowd had gathered. In the centre stood a wooden platform with the execution block draped in black, the axe lying near at hand. A royal official read out the death warrant, though Mary hardly seemed to hear. Carefully her ladies helped her to undress until she was standing in only a dark red petticoat. She forgave all her enemies and told her friends not to weep for her. Then she lay down with her arms outstretched and her head on the block. With a few strokes of his axe the executioner's work was done.

When the news reached Elizabeth, she broke down in tears and fiercely blamed her secretary for making her sign the death warrant. In London people cheered, rang bells and lit bonfires in the streets. In France there was deep mourning. In Scotland some of Mary's friends threatened to march south and burn down Newcastle, but King James did nothing to avenge his mother's execution.

Sixteen years later, in 1603, James got his reward. Elizabeth died and as her nearest Protestant relative, he became King of England and so united the two countries. By then Mary Queen of Scots was long since dead: to some a beautiful she-devil, to others a much-wronged Catholic **martyr**, to historians a failure since she achieved nothing for Scotland, but to most a woman of great mystery.

Things to do

1. Do you think it was wise of Mary to continue to plot for her own release? Had she any other course of action?

2. Read this letter from Elizabeth to Mary's son, James VI, and then write about the view it gives you of Elizabeth's role in the execution:

   'Most Dearly Beloved Brother:
   Would to God you did know, but not feele, with what incomparable sorrow my sad-afflicted heart is troubled, by the late lamentable event, which hapned contrary to my minde and meaning: but because my Penne **abhorreth** the recitall thereof, you shall understand it by this my Kinsman. I beseech you that (as God and many good men are witnesses of my innocencie) you also would believe, that if I had once commanded it, I would never have denyed the same, I am not so base-minded, nor of such a **degenerate** or ignoble spirit, as that either I am affraid to do the thing that is just, or to **disclaime** it being done.
   But as it is most dishonourable in Princes, to cover or colour the **conceptions** of their hearts, in disguised words: So will I never **dissemble** any action of mine, but let it appeare in its owne lively colours. Know this for certainty, that I am as sure, it hapned not by any fault of mine; so if I had ever intended such a deed, I would not have **imputed** it to others. Nor can I assume that to my selfe which I never thought. The rest, the Deliverer of these lines will impart unto you.'

3. Almost every one of Elizabeth's advisers thought the execution necessary. Make a list of reasons why. Do you think they were right? Remember you must try to understand the situation as they saw it in their own times, not as we see it now.

How do we know?

There are official papers such as ambassadors' reports, as well as private papers, including letters, **memoirs** and household accounts. You can read some of the things people wrote about Mary in her own time and later in Ian B. Cowan's *The Enigma of Mary Stewart*. Three modern books about Mary are Antonia Fraser's *Mary Queen of Scots*, Gordon Donaldson's *Mary Queen of Scots* and Rosalind K. Marshall's *Queen of Scots*. This last book is full of beautiful pictures. In all of these books you can see for yourself which sources the authors used.

Most of the books on the Scottish Reformation are very heavy going, but you could look up entries on Knox as well as Luther, Calvin and other Reformers in junior encyclopaedias. You may like to dip into Knox's own *History of the Reformation in Scotland*, edited by W. Croft Dickinson, to get an idea what the man was like from the way he wrote. Knox wrote mainly in English but you can sample the Scots language of the time in Sir David Lindsay's play *A Satire of the Three Estates* in a modern edition by Matthew McDiarmid. A visit to the National Portrait Gallery of Scotland in Edinburgh will show you what many of the people in this book looked like. Next door in the Royal Museum of Scotland you can see some of the things, like guns and furniture, that they used.

Glossary

to **abhor**	to detest
abomination	disgusting behaviour
alliance	agreement for countries to side with each other
ally	member of an alliance
ambassador	person who is sent by one ruler to speak to another
to **avow**	to declare
backgammon	game for two people played on a board with dice and counters
bishop	churchman in charge of priests in a part of the country

to **besiege**	to surround a town or castle with an army
bombardment	attack with heavy guns
bond	agreement
calumny	false and wicked charges
cardinal	high member of the Roman Catholic Church who helps to elect the Pope
casket	small box for keeping valuables like jewels
cavalry	soldiers on horseback
catechism	list of religious beliefs in the form of questions and answers
cathedral	the church of a bishop
commission	body of people appointed to do a certain job
conception	idea
congregation	group of people who worship together
conspirator	plotter
dauphin	title of eldest son of French king: his wife was known as the dauphine
deacon	one who looks after money in a presbyterian church
degenerate	base
disciple	follower of the beliefs of a teacher
to **disdain**	to deny
to **dissemble**	to hide
elder	person who helps a minister to do his job in a presbyterian church
to **excommunicate**	to cut off from the rest of the Church
fliging	dancing
to **forsake**	to abandon
friar	churchman in the Roman Catholic Church who lives like a monk but goes about teaching and preaching
garnet	dark red semi-precious stone
hawking	hunting with hawks for sport
heir	person who inherits what belongs to a dead person
heresy	any religious belief that is different from the Church's teaching
idolatry	worship of idols
illegitimate	born to parents who are not married
to **impute**	to put blame on
intrigue	plot
kin	family
kirk	Scots for church
kirk session	court in a presbyterian church that looks after the business of a parish church
laird	Scots for lord; person who owned land given by the king

Lords of the Congregation	Protestant lords in Scotland at the time of the Reformation
lute	musical instrument with strings that are plucked
martyr	person who suffers death for religious beliefs
mass	religious ceremony in Roman Catholic Church services repeating Christ's Last Supper
massacre	savage killing of many people
memoirs	what a person remembers and writes about his or her own life
moderator	in a prestbyterian church a person who is in charge of a religious gathering
monastery	place where monks live
monk	man who lives according to certain rules in a monastery with others
multitude	crowd
to **muster**	to call together a number of people
nun	woman who lives with others according to certain rules in a nunnery or convent
pamphlet	paperback booklet
partake	share
parish	part of the country with its own priest or minister
pike	weapon consisting of long wooden pole with a point of iron or steel
prestbyterian	to do with a church ruled by 'presbyters' (elders)
priory	small monastery
proclamation	public announcement
rebel	person who rises up to fight a government
to **reform**	to make better by removing faults
regent	person who rules while a king or queen is too young or weak
Reformation	movement for reform in the Catholic Church
to **renounce**	to give up
rude	here a cross
to **sack**	to rob a town
salutary exhortations	helpful advice
satire	poem, play or story which makes fun of people who are wicked or foolish
seigneur	French for lord
sermon	religious speech
stipend	minister's salary
tapestry	heavy cloth hung on a wall

Index